How to Draw
Things in Nature

This book is dedicated to Kandy.

Published in the United States of America by The Child's World®
PO Box 326 • Chanhassen, MN 55317-0326
800-599-READ • www.childsworld.com

Acknowledgments
Design and Production: The Creative Spark, San Juan Capistrano, CA
Series Editor: Elizabeth Sirimarco Budd
Illustration: Rob Court

Library of Congress Cataloging-in-Publication Data
Court, Rob, 1956–
  How to draw things in nature / by Rob Court.
     p. cm. — (The Scribbles Institute)
  ISBN 1-59296-152-5 (library bound : alk. paper)
  1. Nature in art—Juvenile literature. 2. Drawing—Technique—Juvenile
literature. I. Title.
  NC825.N34C68 2004
  743'.7—dc22
                                    2004003733

How to Draw
Things in Nature

Rob Court

The
Child's
World®

It is not enough to believe what you see,
you must also understand what you see.

—Leonardo da Vinci

Parents and Teachers,

Children love to draw! It is an essential part of a child's
learning process. Drawing skills are used to investigate both
natural and constructed environments, record observations,
solve problems, and express ideas. The purpose of this book is
to help students advance through the challenges of drawing and
to encourage the use of drawing in school projects. The reader
is also introduced to the elements of visual art—lines, shapes,
patterns, form, texture, light, space, and color—and their
importance in the fundamentals of drawing.

The Scribbles Institute is devoted to educational materials
that keep creativity in our schools and in our children's dreams.
Our mission is to empower young creative thinkers with knowledge
in visual art while helping to improve their drawing skills.
Students, parents, and teachers are invited to visit our Web
site—www.scribblesinstitute.com—for useful information and
guidance. You can even get advice from a drawing coach!

Contents

Drawing Things in Nature

It's exciting to draw things in nature! You can draw a giant pine tree while hiking in the mountains. You can draw a mysterious wolf or a friendly frog while looking at photographs. Or you can draw a beautiful flower from your imagination.

The easy steps in this book will help you draw things in nature for school projects or for fun. Find a big piece of paper and a pencil. You can get started right now!

On the Move!
Things in nature are always moving. Try to sketch lines showing a tree bending in the wind or how its branches twist and turn as they grow toward the sun. With practice, you'll be able to draw guidelines showing the movement of a bird's wings.

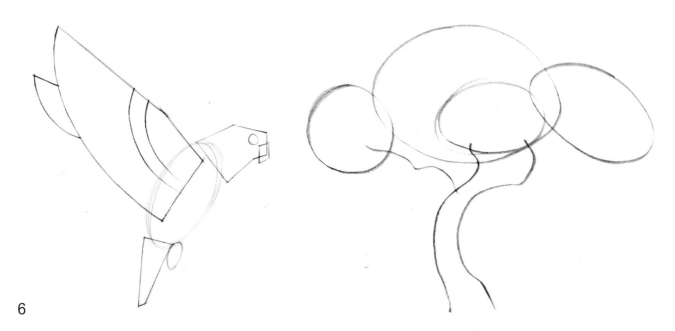

Shown above are pages from Rob Court's sketchbook. He had plenty of time to draw details of a tree on a cold, wintery day, but only a few minutes to sketch the form of his dog before she woke up and changed position.

Your Sketchbook

Artists always have a sketchbook nearby. A sketch is a quick drawing that shows the basic form of something in nature. Later you might use your sketch to create a more detailed drawing. A sketchbook is a great place to keep ideas for your art projects. You can practice the lessons on the following pages in your sketchbook, too.

Drawing with Shapes

Drawing things in nature is easy when you start with basic shapes. Shapes show the petals of a flower. Sketch these shapes lightly. Then you can erase them later as you finish your picture.

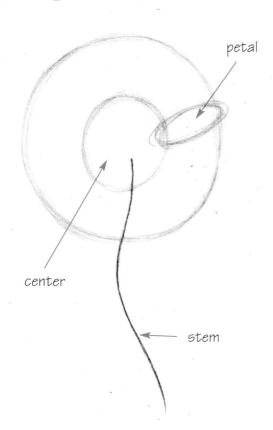

petal

center

stem

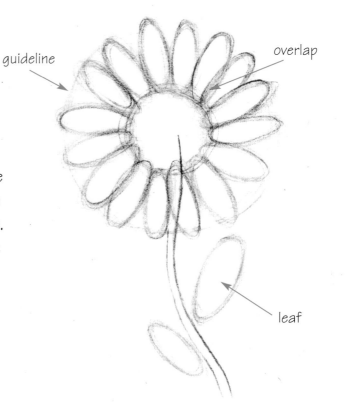

Flower

1 Start by sketching a circle for the center of the flower. Next draw an oval shape for a petal. Notice how it overlaps the center. Sketch a larger circle as a guideline around the outside tip of the petal.

guideline

overlap

leaf

2 The guideline will help you make all the petals about the same size. Continue by drawing more petals, as shown at right. Overlap the ovals to show how petals rest on top of each other. Use curved lines for the stem and oval shapes for the leaves.

Drawing with Lines

Drawing an **outline** around the edge of the shapes you've made forms the flower. Keep drawing until you like the outline. Remember to draw lightly so that you can erase if you need to.

3. Take time to look at the shapes you've drawn for the flower. Do you like what you've drawn? Continue by carefully drawing an outline around the shapes. Draw lines that show petals overlapping each other. Some petals are almost hidden behind others. Next, draw the outlines for the stem and leaves. Notice how the leaves are shaped differently from the petals.

hidden behind other petals

4. Using angled and curved lines, draw a darker outline to finish your picture. Draw lines to show the edges and folds of the petals. To draw the center, repeat small circles to make a pattern. Carefully draw the curved lines for the stem and the edges of the leaves.

You can draw many things in nature with shapes and lines. A dragonfly is an insect with a long, narrow body and **transparent** wings.

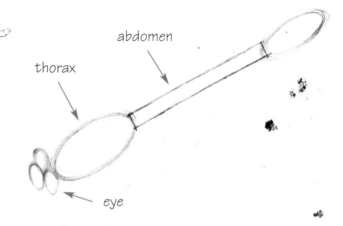

Dragonfly

1 Insects' bodies are divided into three sections: the head, thorax, and abdomen. Start by lightly sketching ovals for the head and thorax. A long, narrow rectangle forms the abdomen, or the tail area. Draw three small ovals for its eyes and head.

thorax

abdomen

eye

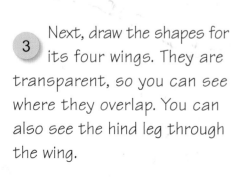

2 The center part, or thorax, has three pairs of legs and two pairs of wings. Notice how lines are used for its feet. Sketch three ovals at the front of the thorax.

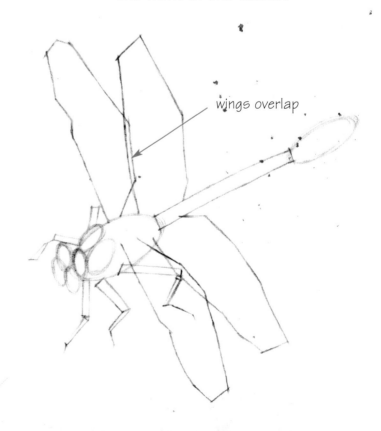

wings overlap

3 Next, draw the shapes for its four wings. They are transparent, so you can see where they overlap. You can also see the hind leg through the wing.

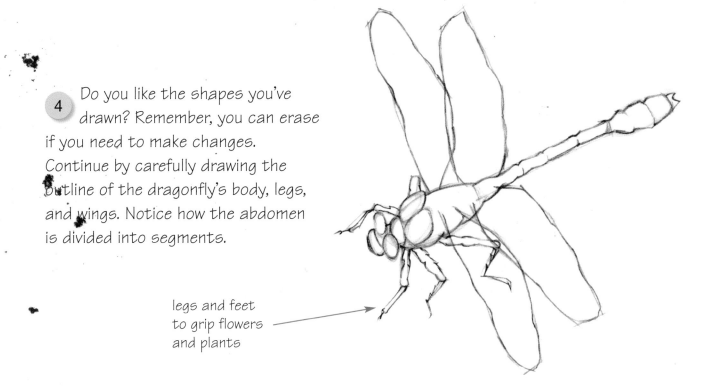

4 Do you like the shapes you've drawn? Remember, you can erase if you need to make changes. Continue by carefully drawing the outline of the dragonfly's body, legs, and wings. Notice how the abdomen is divided into segments.

legs and feet to grip flowers and plants

5 With a darker pencil, draw the outlines to finish the dragonfly's body. Include details such as its face, triangular shapes on its back, and the outlines of its legs. Lightly draw the edges and patterns of the wings.

HOT TIP **Thin Lines**

Use a thicker, bold outline for the body of the dragonfly. Use a thin line to show the edges and patterns of the transparent wings. Notice the difference between the thicker and thinner lines. See page 25 to learn more about different pencils.

11

Patterns

You can create patterns by repeating lines or shapes. Draw the pattern on the wings of a butterfly.

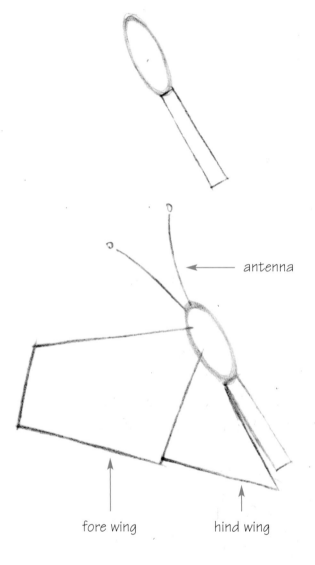

Butterfly

1 Like a dragonfly, the butterfly has a long and narrow body. Start by sketching an oval and rectangle.

2 Using straight lines, lightly sketch the guidelines for its wings. Notice how the wings connect to the body. Now add two curved lines and two dots for the antennas.

antenna

fore wing   hind wing

3 Next, carefully match the angles of the guidelines of the wings on both sides of the body. To check your drawing, compare the size of the wings on both sides.

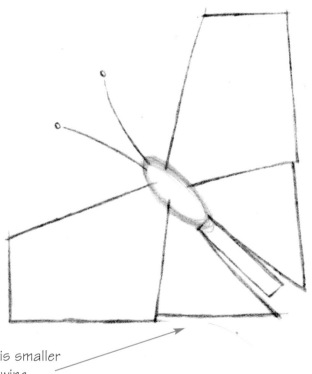

The hind wing is smaller than the fore wing.

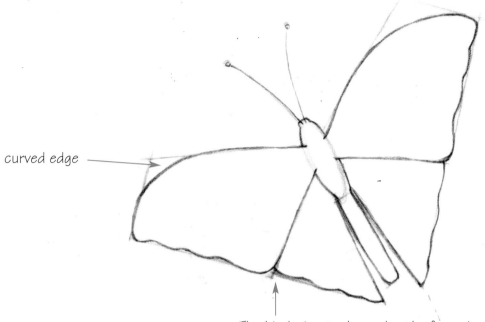

curved edge

The hind wing tucks under the fore wing.

4   Using the guidelines, carefully draw the outlines of the wings. Notice where the edges of the wings are curved inside the guidelines. Draw the outlines for its body.

5   Draw the darker outlines that show the wings and body of the butterfly. Next, draw the lines for the patterns on its wings. Draw one side and then the other, making sure to match the patterns on both sides. Notice how certain lines and shapes are repeated to create the patterns. Add the pattern of lines on its abdomen.

Three-Dimensional Form

With practice, you can change flat shapes into three-dimensional or "3-D" forms. Start drawing a wolf by making ovals for its body and head.

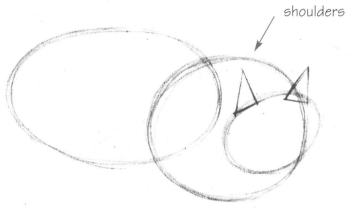

shoulders

Wolf

1 Sketch an oval for the shoulders and chest area. Next, draw a smaller oval for the head. Draw two triangular shapes for the ears. A long oval creates the torso area.

2 This wolf is walking in snow, looking for its next meal. Sketch the shapes for the front and rear legs. An oval shows the powerful thigh. Draw circles to show the ankle and leg joints. Next, draw the shapes for its paws. Continue by drawing the shape for the face. Two small ovals are the eyes. Add the shape for the tail and lines for the snowy ground.

thigh

tail

eye

ankle joint

paw hidden in snow

contour line
shows rear leg

nose

paw

3 See how the lines of the fur coat follow the form of the wolf's body. These are called **contour** lines. Carefully draw contour lines that form the body, legs, and head. Include details such as the eyes, nose, ears, and mouth. Don't forget to draw the bushy tail. Take a moment to compare your picture to the wolf shown above. Do you like the contour lines that you've drawn? Keep drawing until you like the form of the wolf. You can make changes if you need to.

4 Finish your picture by carefully drawing the darker outlines of the wolf. Take care to include details for the fur coat, leg muscles, and teeth. See how the fur is longer and hangs down around the chest and belly. It is shorter and stands up on the wolf's shoulders and back.

spine

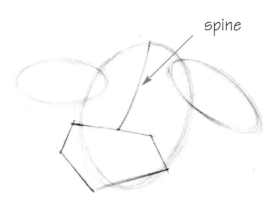

Frog

1. Lightly sketch an oval for the body. Begin drawing the strong rear legs by making ovals. Next, sketch the shape for the head. A lightly drawn line forms the spine.

2. Continue by drawing two longer ovals for the legs. See how the shapes overlap on each leg. Add two small ovals for the eyes. The shape of the eye on the left is different because the head is turned slightly.

Overlapping shows this part of the leg is behind the other.

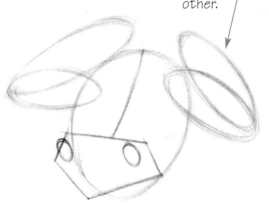

Guidelines show where to draw the feet.

3. Sketch the shapes that form the large rear feet. Notice how they are hidden behind the legs. Sketch the shapes for the front legs. Then carefully sketch the shapes of its front feet. Inside the guidelines, start sketching the shape of the head. Continue sketching until you like the shapes you've drawn.

16

contour line

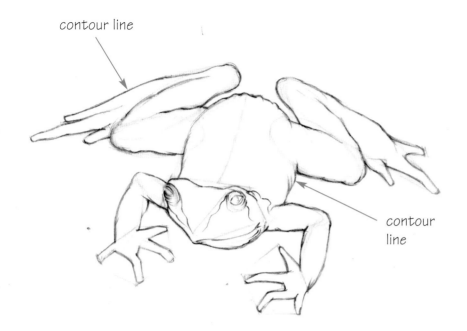

Foreshortening

Take a moment to look at the picture at left. Notice how the body is drawn behind the head. The feet are drawn behind the legs. The frog's body looks as if it is coming toward you. Drawing in this way is called foreshortening.

contour line

4 Carefully draw the outlines that make the frog look three-dimensional. Draw contour lines to show the roundness of the powerful legs and large eyes. Contour lines create strong feet made for climbing tree branches.

5 With a darker pencil, draw the outlines to finish your picture. Notice how bumps on the skin are shown with contour lines. The way the frog's skin feels is called texture. To learn more about texture, see page 26. Patterns on the skin are created by drawing angled and curved lines.

Contour lines show the roundness of the legs.

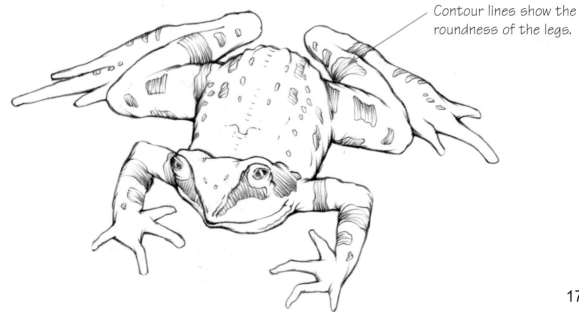

An Artist's View of Trees

There are many kinds of trees in nature. When you take the time to look at trees, you'll find interesting details to draw.

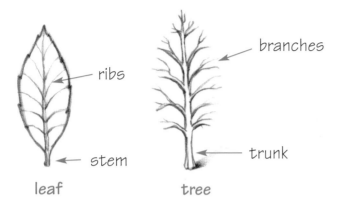

leaf

tree

Leaves are attached to small, flexible branches. Use curved lines when drawing the smaller branches.

Look at a leaf from a tree. The ribs of a leaf flow outward, the same as the branches of the tree.

Trees and bushes spring from the ground like water from a fountain.

Small branches are carried toward the sun by larger ones. When drawing, notice how branches are connected to each other.

Drawing every leaf of a tree can take a long time! Artists use different **techniques** to show large groups

A tree has branches on all sides. To get an idea, hold your arm out in front of you. Open your hand as if it is holding a bowl. Now, imagine your arm as the tree's trunk and your fingers as its branches. Turn your hand and see how the branches spread upward and away from the trunk.

or masses of leaves. One technique is to draw only a small number of leaves and then draw lines to show a large mass.

Branches at the top of the pine tree are smaller and point upward.

Some branches are behind the tree.

Some branches are in front of the tree, pointing toward you.

Larger branches at the bottom point downward.

Branches can be hidden by masses of leaves.

Lines show the rough and bumpy surface of the tree.

tree root

Point of View

Sketching a tree outdoors can be fun! Position yourself far enough away to draw the height of the whole tree. Sit closer if you want to see details such as branches and leaves.

HOT TIP

Sometimes artists want to quickly sketch the form of a tree. A technique for showing the roundness of the trunk and branches is to draw bracelet lines.

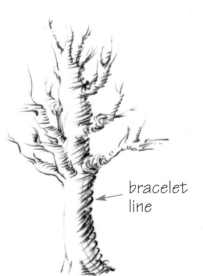

bracelet line

The Life of a Tree

The form of a tree can tell you a lot about its history. Some trees are bent by the wind, and some need to twist and turn as they grow toward sunlight. Draw the lines that show the direction the tree is growing.

Light and Shadows

By using light and dark **tones,** you can create shadows. Drawing shadows helps you see the form of a tree and the ground underneath it.

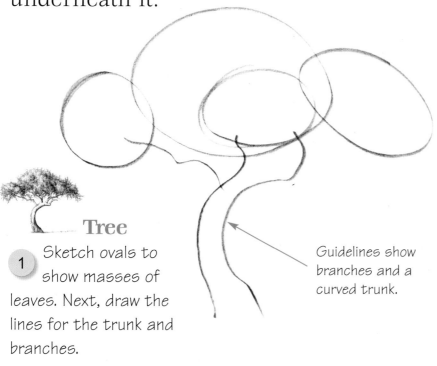

Tree

1 Sketch ovals to show masses of leaves. Next, draw the lines for the trunk and branches.

Guidelines show branches and a curved trunk.

Some branches are behind others or hidden by masses of leaves.

2 Take time to draw the outlines for the leaves. Next, carefully outline the trunk and branches. Press lightly with your pencil when drawing your outlines. This makes it easier to erase the shapes before drawing the shadows shown in step 4.

Light Source

Places where light comes from are called light sources. The sun is a light source. A lamp is also a light source. In the drawing below, a light source shines on a sphere. How do the shadows change as the light changes position?

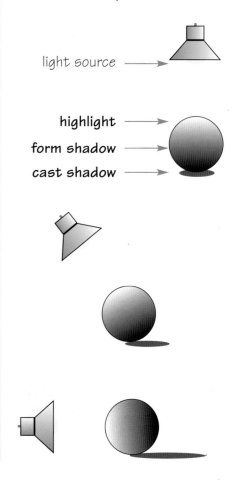

light source

highlight

form shadow

cast shadow

3 Before adding shadows, carefully draw darker outlines that form the trunk and branches. Draw contour lines to show their roundness. Add lines that show the texture of the branches and trunk. Continue by drawing the areas with leaves. When you like what you've drawn, carefully erase your guidelines.

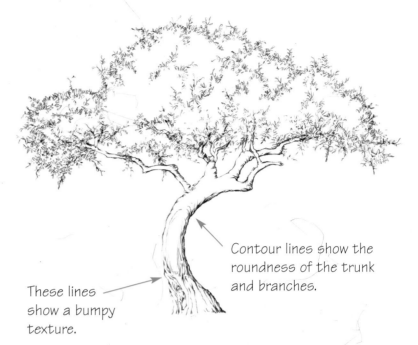

Contour lines show the roundness of the trunk and branches.

These lines show a bumpy texture.

4 Start drawing shadows in areas where no light shines from the light source. Hold your pencil on its side, press firmly, and begin drawing the darkest shadows on the tree. Shadows are lighter where more light touches it. Use less pressure on your pencil as you draw lighter shadows. Fade the shadows away to the white of the paper where there are highlights. Remember to draw the cast shadow on the ground, to the right of the tree.

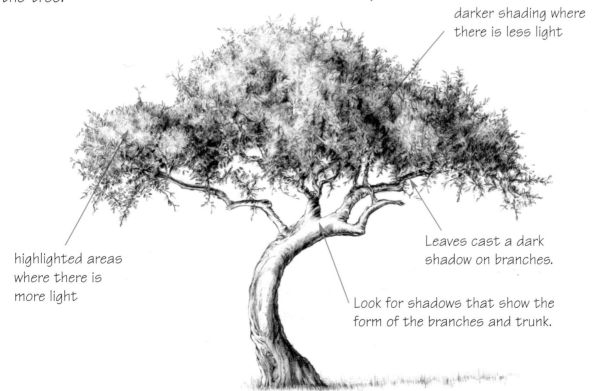

darker shading where there is less light

highlighted areas where there is more light

Leaves cast a dark shadow on branches.

Look for shadows that show the form of the branches and trunk.

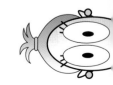

Space and Composition

The white space of your paper can be transformed into a landscape with a road and trees. The way you divide the space is called composition.

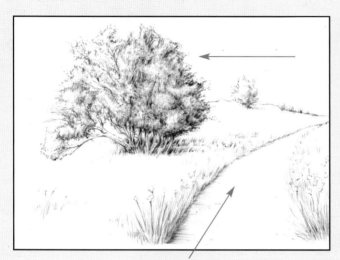

direction your eye travels

Travel into a Landscape

Composition makes your landscape more interesting to look at. See how the flowers and road lead your eye into the picture. The horizon line divides the space between the ground and sky. Smaller trees and the horizon line direct your eye to the larger tree at left. Notice how the shadows on the tree and ground direct your eye to the center of the composition.

Country Landscape

1 Begin by drawing the horizon line. It shows the hills in the distance. Next, draw the curved lines for the road. Notice how the lines are closer together toward the horizon line. Lightly sketch the shapes for the trees. Add lines for the trunks and branches. The tree closest to you is larger.

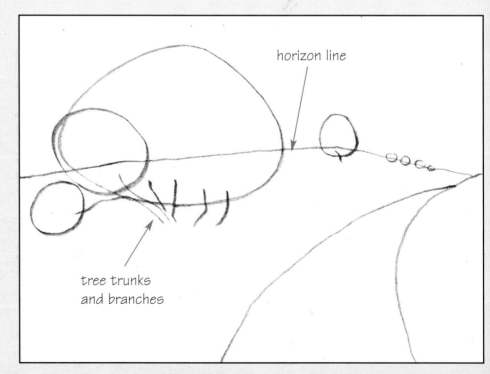

horizon line

tree trunks and branches

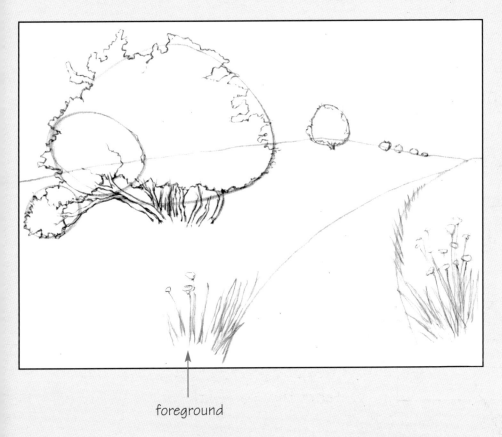

foreground

2 Lightly sketch the flowers. They are in the space closest to you, which is called the foreground. Add the tall grass along the road. Next, draw the outlines of the areas with leaves. Continue with the outlines for the tree trunks and branches.

background

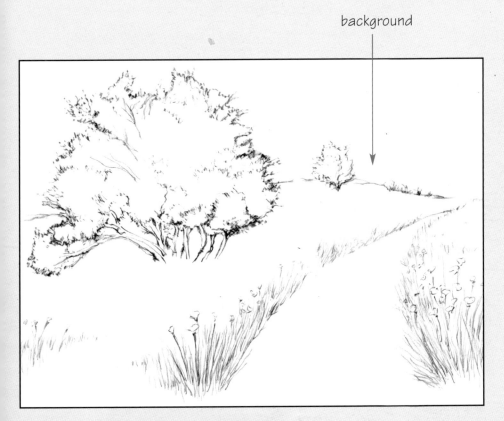

3 Carefully draw the darker, final outlines that form the trees. Remember, you don't have to draw every leaf! Draw just enough to show an area of leaves. Add details such as the grass and flowers in the foreground. Use fewer lines to draw things that are far away, in the background. See how simple lines are used for grass in the distance and a group of trees on the horizon line.

23

4 Take time to look at the outlines you have drawn. Do they show the flowers in the foreground? Can you see where leaves overlap branches on the trees? Continue by drawing the darkest shadows that the trees cast on the ground. Also draw the shadows that the flowers cast.

Shadows move away from the light source.

5 Next, draw shadows that form large masses of leaves. To do this, turn your pencil on its side and begin shading areas facing away from the light source. Use a lighter gray tone in areas where the light source shines. Add shadows on the ground. To finish your picture, draw darker lines for details such as leaves, branches, and flowers.

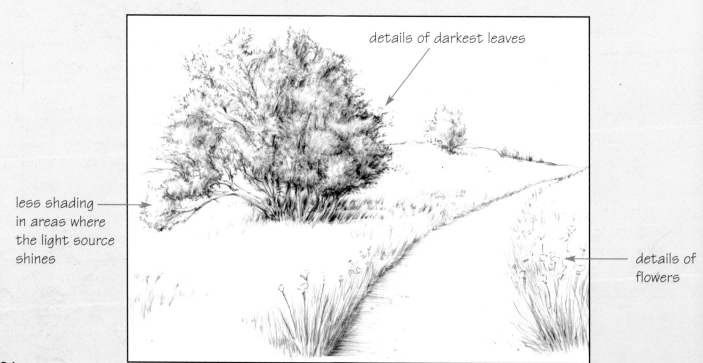

details of darkest leaves

less shading in areas where the light source shines

details of flowers

Which Pencil Should You Use?

A standard "2B" or "2SOFT"' pencil works well for most drawings, but other pencils can make your drawing even more interesting.

Pencils are numbered according to how hard or soft the lead is. You'll find this number written on the pencil. A number combined with the letter "H" means the lead is hard (2H, 3H, 4H, etc.). When you draw with hard leads, the larger the number you use, the lighter and thinner your lines will be.

A number combined with the letter "B" means the lead is soft (2B, 4B, 6B, etc.). The lines you draw will get darker and thicker with larger numbers. Sometimes you will read "2SOFT" or "2B" on standard pencils used for schoolwork. When you see the letter "F" on a pencil, it means the pencil is of medium hardness.

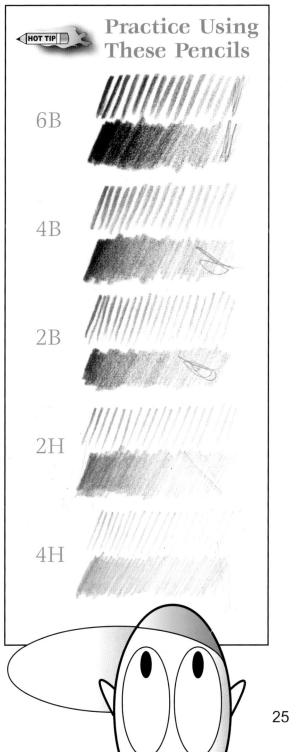

Practice Using These Pencils

HOT TIP

6B

4B

2B

2H

4H

Texture

How the surface of something feels is called texture. The texture of a leaf is different from the texture of wood or a rock. You can draw lines and patterns to create different textures.

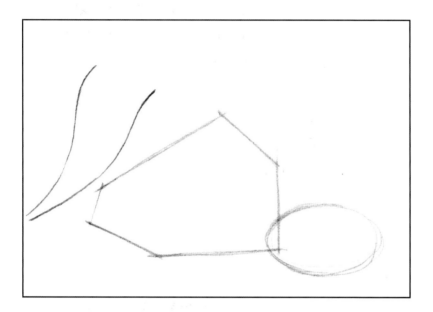

Butterfly in the Forest

1 Begin your composition by drawing the shapes for the rocks. One has angles, and the other is round. Next, draw two curved lines for the plant.

2 Continue by drawing the shapes for leaves. In the background, sketch lines for a tree that has fallen to the ground. It is behind the rock. Notice how the leaf overlaps the rock. Add the shapes for the butterfly. Turn to page 12 to learn to draw the butterfly.

guidelines for tree branch

The leaf and rock overlap.

Take time to look at your composition. Do you like the shapes that you've drawn?
Do you like how they are positioned in the picture?

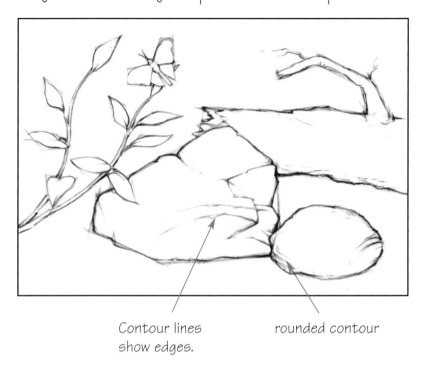

Contour lines
show edges.

rounded contour

3 Carefully draw the outlines around the shapes that you've drawn. Begin making contour lines to show the form of the rocks.

4 Finish your picture by carefully drawing the darker outlines that form the plant, butterfly, rocks, and tree.

Begin adding the short, angular lines that show texture on the larger rock. Darken its contour lines to show edges of the rock. Next, add dots and lines to show texture on the smaller rock. Notice how the texture follows the curved contour lines. Draw the lines to show the texture of the tree. Draw thicker, darker lines to show the shaded area, close to the ground. Add final details such as grass and the shadows the rocks cast.

The tree has a rough edge.

texture lines

Drawing with Color

By using colored pencils, you can make a drawing of a parakeet more exciting. Create the colors of its body and wings by mixing yellow, blue, red, and black.

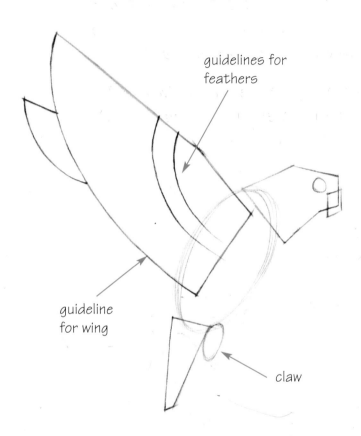

guidelines for feathers

guideline for wing

claw

Parakeet

1 Start by sketching an oval for the body. Next, draw guidelines for outstretched wings. Notice how one wing is behind the other. Include guidelines for drawing the feathers. See how the wings connect to the body. Draw shapes for the head and beak. Make a circle for the eye. Draw a triangular shape for the tail and an oval for the claw.

2 Begin sketching the outlines of the head, body, and tail. Carefully draw the contours of the beak and claw. Notice how the angles of the feathers form the outstretched wings. Take time to draw outlines for the feathers, showing where they overlap. Some are longer than others. Add outlines for the eye.

Feathers closer to the body are shorter.

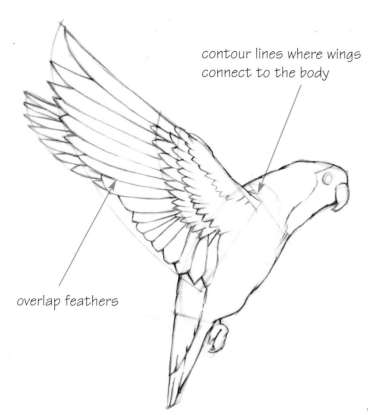

contour lines where wings connect to the body

overlap feathers

3 Continue by drawing the darker outlines that form the parakeet. Carefully draw outlines for the larger and smaller feathers. Take a moment to look at what you've drawn. Do you like the way the feathers overlap?

When you like the lines you've drawn, carefully erase all guidelines and prepare to add color.

Adding one color on top of another in a drawing is called layering. To learn how to layer primary colors, try using only yellow, blue, red, as well as black, in this drawing.

4 Start by lightly shading the body and beak with a yellow pencil. Think about the direction from where the light source is shining. Apply more pressure to darken areas where there are shadows. Continue by shading the part of the parakeet's wing that is yellow. Notice the darker yellow areas on the neck and under the wing.

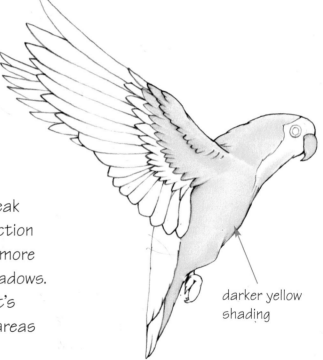

darker yellow shading

Primary Colors

red   yellow   blue

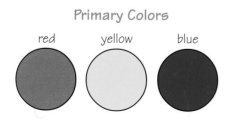

Secondary Colors

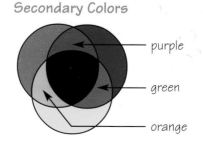

purple

green

orange

Mixing primary colors creates secondary colors.

29

mix blue over yellow

5 Next, add a layer of light blue over the yellow areas of the body and wing. Make the blue darker in areas where there are more shadows, such as under the wing. What color do you get when you mix blue with yellow? Continue by lightly shading the feathers of the wings with blue. Areas where wings overlap are a darker shade of blue.

Mixing Colored Pencils Is Fun!

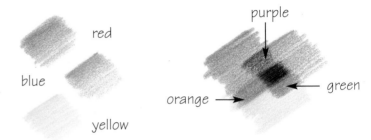

red

blue

yellow

purple

orange

green

6 Fun things start to happen when you add red to this drawing. Lightly shade the parakeet's face with red. Add a layer of light red on the feathers and back. What color do you get when you add red on top of the yellow areas? Remember to make darker shadows that are farther away from the light source.

Shading with black creates the 3-D form of the body, wings, and claw. Highlights and shadows add realistic details, such as the feathers and the back of the head.

mix red over blue

highlight

30

The Artist's Studio

Artists need a special place where they can relax and concentrate on their work.

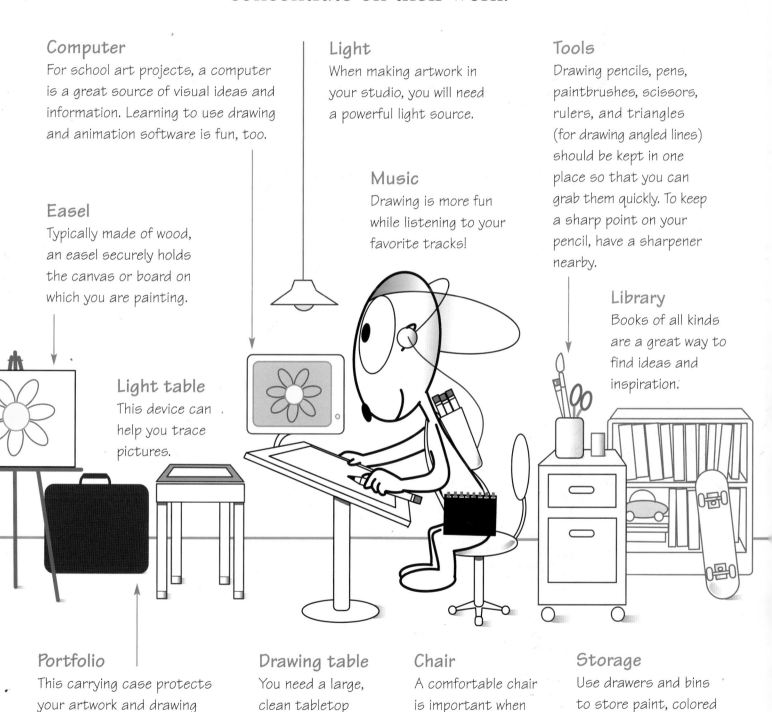

Computer
For school art projects, a computer is a great source of visual ideas and information. Learning to use drawing and animation software is fun, too.

Easel
Typically made of wood, an easel securely holds the canvas or board on which you are painting.

Light
When making artwork in your studio, you will need a powerful light source.

Music
Drawing is more fun while listening to your favorite tracks!

Tools
Drawing pencils, pens, paintbrushes, scissors, rulers, and triangles (for drawing angled lines) should be kept in one place so that you can grab them quickly. To keep a sharp point on your pencil, have a sharpener nearby.

Library
Books of all kinds are a great way to find ideas and inspiration.

Light table
This device can help you trace pictures.

Portfolio
This carrying case protects your artwork and drawing tablets.

Drawing table
You need a large, clean tabletop on which to draw.

Chair
A comfortable chair is important when you spend a lot of time drawing.

Storage
Use drawers and bins to store paint, colored pencils, pastels, and other supplies.

Glossary

A **cast shadow** is the shadow that a person, animal, or object throws on the ground, a wall, or other feature.

A **contour** is the outline of something; in your drawings, a contour line follows the natural shape of things in nature.

A **form shadow** is a shadow in a drawing that shows the form or shape of a person, animal, or object.

A **highlight** is the area (or areas) in a drawing that receives the most light from the light source.

An **outline** is a line that shows the shape of an object, animal, or person.

Techniques are special methods or ways of doing something.

Tones are lighter and darker shades of a color.

You can see through something that is **transparent.**

Index

About the Author

Rob Court is a designer and illustrator. He started the Scribbles Institute™ to help people learn about the importance of drawing and visual art.